T G R

YAZAR: ECE İ. GÜNDOĞAN
EDİTÖR: SERDAR KAPLAN
ILLUSTRASYON: TOLGA BEDÜK
SAYFA DÜZENİ: EZGİ S. SEKMEN
YAYIMA HAZIRLAYAN: AHMET KAPLAN

BASKI: 1. BASKI / ŞUBAT 2024

TGR YAYINCILIK CAFERAĞA MAH. NEŞET ÖMER SOKAK NO
11/3A KADIKÖY–İSTANBUL TEL: 0216 450 1170
WWW.TGRYAYİNCİLİK.COM İNFO@TGRYAYİNCİLİK.COM
SERTİFİKA NO: 71627

BASKI: UNIFSET BASIM YAYIN SAN. VE TİC. LTD. ŞTİ.
YAKUPLU MAH. 194. SOK. NO:1/159 3. MATBAACILAR SİTESİ
BEYLİKDÜZÜ / İSTANBUL – TEL: 0212 875 37 85
SERTİFİKA NO: 72541

ISBN: 9786259432595

T G R

Sherlock and Timmy's Toys

TGR

ADVENTURE IS STARTING!

I am Doctor Watson. I live on Baker Street with my friend Sherlock. Sherlock's job is very exciting. He is the world's smartest detective. Sherlock's favorite belongings are his long brown coat and his magnifying glass.

One day, Timmy, a nine-year-old child, came to our house crying.

Timmy lives in a house with a garden at the end of the street. Sometimes, Sherlock goes to his house and tells him detective stories. Sherlock asked, "What happened, Timmy? Why are you crying?" Timmy said, "Someone stole my toys." Sherlock replied, "Calm down and tell me the story."

Last night, I was playing games in my room. I took out my blue, green, and red toy cars from the game box. I sat on the floor and was driving them.

My mother invited me to dinner in the evening.
So, I went to the kitchen to eat.

When I returned to my room, all of my toys were gone.

Sherlock started thinking. "Did anyone else come to the house for dinner yesterday?" Timmy replied, "No, it was just my mom and me," Sherlock said, "We need to go to the scene of the incident."

When we went to Timmy's room, Sherlock immediately started collecting clues. The room was on the ground floor, but the window was closed. Sherlock said, "Interesting." There was a broken vase on the floor, and the toys weren't here. There were also muddy footprints on the floor. Sherlock looked out of the window and said, "Let's examine the garden!"

There were muddy footprints in the garden. The tracks were leading to the neighbor's garden.

Timmy pointed to that place and said, "That's Tom and his family's house. Tom took my toys." Sherlock replied, "Don't be so sure; we didn't solve the case yet."

Sherlock and Timmy went to Tom and his family's house.
Timmy rang the doorbell.

Tom opened the door and was very surprised to see Timmy and Sherlock. Sherlock said, "Last night, Timmy's toys went missing, and there were footprints in the garden. The same footprints are in your house's garden too. Did you see Timmy's toys?"

We went to my grandpa's for a vacation. We just returned this morning, so I didn't see any toys," he said. Sherlock replied, "I know." Tom asked, "How do you know?" Sherlock said, "This morning when I came to Timmy's house, I saw you and your family. You had suitcases with you, and your mailbox was full. This shows you were away for a long time.

Sherlock asked, "Do you have a dog in your garden?" Tom replied, "Yes, I have a dog in the backyard. He's my best friend. His name is Bobby." Sherlock said, "Can you take me to Bobby?"

When we went to Bobby's kennel, Timmy's toys were inside the kennel. Timmy was very happy. Sherlock solved the case and began to explain.

Bobby was alone for three days and got bored. He went to Timmy's to play, but Timmy was having dinner with his mother. He entered Timmy's room through an open window, took his toys, and brought them to his kennel. Bobby played with the toys all night.

Timmy felt very embarrassed because he thought his friend had taken the toys. Timmy realized his mistake and said sorry to Tom. Sherlock held Timmy's hand and led him back home.

ACTIVITIES

Mark the statements as True (T) or False (F).

1. SHERLOCK HOLMES IS A DETECTIVE. ( )
2. SHERLOCK HOLMES AND DOCTOR WATSON LIVE TOGETHER. ( )
3. THERE WERE MUDDY FOOTPRINTS IN TOM'S GARDEN. ( )
4. TIMMY LIVES IN AN APARTMENT AT THE END OF THE STREET. ( )
5. TOM WAS THE ONE WHO TOOK TIMMY'S TOYS. ( )
6. SHERLOCK ADVISED TIMMY TO CALM DOWN AND SHARE THE STORY. ( )
7. THE MUDDY FOOTPRINTS LED TO TOM'S HOUSE. ( )
8. TIMMY'S MOTHER WAS WITH HIM WHEN HE WAS HAVING DINNER. ( )
9. TIMMY AND SHERLOCK WENT TO TOM'S HOUSE TO FIND THE MISSING TOYS. ( )
10. BOBBY PLAYED WITH TOM'S TOYS ALL NIGHT. ( )

Find the hidden words below.

K	E	N	N	E	L	A	E	T	V	S	C	A	S	U	V
E	D	O	T	N	M	S	B	N	D	O	G	O	L	C	A
S	O	S	K	V	I	E	C	G	U	L	K	M	D	B	C
S	O	U	O	I	S	T	A	C	S	V	D	I	K	D	A
G	E	L	M	V	T	T	O	E	C	A	S	E	A	S	T
S	V	G	V	N	A	S	E	T	K	L	T	N	G	O	I
H	U	O	K	E	K	F	A	M	C	R	U	N	D	V	O
M	E	S	V	D	E	T	E	C	T	I	V	E	A	T	N

MISTAKE
DOG
DETECTIVE
SOLVE
KENNEL
CASE
VACATION
CLUE

TOYS KENNEL MAGNIFYING GLASS FOOTPRINTS

____

____

____

____

ALONE MISTAKE MAILBOX DOORBELL KENNEL

1. Timmy's toys were found in Bobby's ______________.
2. Bobby took Timmy's toys because he was ______________.
3. Timmy realized his ______________ and said sorry to Tom.
4. Sherlock observed suitcases and a full ______________.
5. Sherlock and Timmy went to Tom's house, and Timmy rang the ______________.

Mark the best option.

1. Who is Sherlock?
a) A teacher
b) A doctor
c) The world's smartest detective
d) A chef

2. What are Sherlock's favorite belongings?
a) A hat and a cane
b) A long brown coat and a magnifying glass
c) A notebook and a pencil
d) A laptop and a phone

3. Who came to Sherlock's house crying?
a) A neighbor
b) Timmy, a nine-year-old child
c) Tom
d) Timmy's mother

4. Where does Timmy live?
a) In an apartment
b) In a house with a garden at the end of the street
c) In a hotel
d) On Baker Street

5. What happened to Timmy's toys?
a) They were broken
b) They were lost
c) They were stolen
d) They were given away

6. What colors were Timmy's toy cars?
a) Blue, green, and red
b) Yellow, black, and white
c) Orange, purple, and pink
d) Brown, grey, and silver

7. Where were muddy footprints found?
a) In the kitchen
b) In the garden
c) On the sofa
d) In the bathroom

8. Who did Timmy initially think took his toys?
a) His mother
b) Tom and his family
c) Sherlock
d) The mailman

9. What did Sherlock observe about Tom's family?
a) They were having a party
b) They just returned from a vacation
c) They were moving out
d) They were renovating their house

10. Who actually took Timmy's toys?
a) Tom
b) Timmy's mother
c) Bobby, Tom's dog
d) A stranger

Answer Key

1. SHERLOCK HOLMES IS A DETECTIVE. (T)
2. SHERLOCK HOLMES AND DOCTOR WATSON LIVE TOGETHER. (T)
3. THERE WERE MUDDY FOOTPRINTS IN THE GARDEN. (T)
4. TIMMY LIVES IN AN APARTMENT AT THE END OF THE STREET. (F)
5. TOM WAS THE ONE WHO TOOK TIMMY'S TOYS. (F)
6. SHERLOCK ADVISED TIMMY TO CALM DOWN AND SHARE THE STORY. (T)
7. THE MUDDY FOOTPRINTS LED TO TOM'S HOUSE. (T)
8. TIMMY'S MOTHER WAS WITH HIM WHEN HE WAS HAVING DINNER. (T)
9. TIMMY AND SHERLOCK WENT TO TOM'S HOUSE TO FIND THE MISSING TOYS
10. BOBBY PLAYED WITH TOM'S TOYS ALL NIGHT. (F)

K	E	N	N	E	L	A	E	T	V	S	C	A	S	U	V
E	D	O	T	N	M	S	B	N	D	O	G	O	L	C	A
S	O	S	K	V	I	E	C	G	U	L	K	M	D	B	C
S	O	U	O	I	S	T	A	C	S	V	D	I	K	D	A
G	E	L	M	V	T	T	O	E	C	A	S	E	A	S	T
S	V	G	V	N	A	S	E	T	K	L	T	N	G	O	I
H	U	O	K	E	K	F	A	M	C	R	U	N	D	V	O
M	E	S	V	D	E	T	E	C	T	I	V	E	A	T	N

MISTAKE
DOG
DETECTIVE
SOLVE
~~KENNEL~~
CASE
VACATION
CLUE

magnifying glass

footprints

toys

kennel

1. Timmy's toys were found in Bobby's kennel.
2. Bobby took Timmy's toys because he was alone.
3. Timmy realized his mistake and said sorry to Tom.
4. Sherlock observed suitcases and a full mailbox.
5. Sherlock and Timmy went to Tom's house, and Timmy rang the doorbell.

1C - 2B - 3B - 4B - 5C 6A - 7B - 8B - 9B - 10C